Table Layout in CSS

Eric A. Meyer

Beijing · Boston · Farnham · Sebastopol · Tokyo

Table Layout in CSS

by Eric A. Meyer

Printed in the United States of America.

Published by O'Reilly Media, Inc., 1005 Gravenstein Highway North, Sebastopol, CA 95472.

O'Reilly books may be purchased for educational, business, or sales promotional use. Online editions are also available for most titles (*http://safaribooksonline.com*). For more information, contact our corporate/institutional sales department: 800-998-9938 or *corporate@oreilly.com*.

Editor: Meg Foley	**Interior Designer:** David Futato
Production Editor: Colleen Lobner	**Cover Designer:** Randy Comer
Copyeditor: Molly Ives Brower	**Illustrator:** Rebecca Demarest
Proofreader: Amanda Kersey	

June 2016:   First Edition

Revision History for the First Edition
2016-06-08:   First Release

See *http://oreilly.com/catalog/errata.csp?isbn=9781491930533* for release details.

978-1-491-93053-3

[LSI]

Table of Contents

Table Layout in CSS

You may have glanced at that title and wondered, "Table layout? Isn't that exactly what we're trying to *avoid* doing?" Indeed so, but this chapter is not about using tables *for* layout. Instead, it's about the ways that tables themselves are laid out by CSS, which is a far more complicated affair than it might first appear.

Tables are unusual, compared to the rest of document layout. Until flexbox and grid came along, tables alone possessed the unique ability to associate element sizes with other elements—for example, all the cells in a row have the same height, no matter how much or how little content each individual cell might contain. The same is true for the widths of cells that share a column. Cells that adjoin can share a border, even if the two cells have very different border styles. As we'll see, these abilities are purchased at the expense of a great many behaviors and rules—many of them rooted deep in the past—that apply to tables, and only tables.

Table Formatting

Before we can start to worry about how cell borders are drawn and tables sized, we need to delve into the fundamental ways in which tables are assembled, and the ways that elements within a table are related. This is referred to as *table formatting*, and it is quite distinct from table layout: the layout is possible only after the formatting has been completed.

Visually Arranging a Table

The first thing to understand is how CSS defines the arrangement of tables. While this knowledge may seem a bit basic, it's key to understanding how best to style tables.

CSS draws a distinction between *table elements* and *internal table elements*. In CSS, internal table elements generate rectangular boxes that have content, padding, and borders, but not margins. Therefore, it is *not* possible to define the separation between table cells by giving them margins. A CSS-conformant browser will ignore any attempts to apply margins to cells, rows, or any other internal table element (with the exception of captions, which are discussed in the section "Captions" on page 14).

There are six basic rules for arranging tables. The basis of these rules is a *grid cell*, which is one area between the grid lines on which a table is drawn. Consider Figure 1, in which two tables are shown: their grid cells are indicated by the dashed lines drawn over the tables.

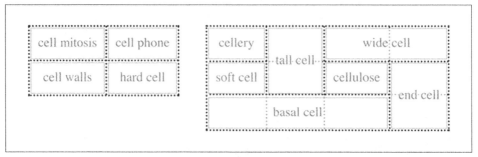

Figure 1. Grid cells form the basis of table layout

In a simple two-by-two table, such as the lefthand table shown in Figure 1, the grid cells correspond to the actual table cells. In a more complicated table, like the right-hand table in Figure 1, some table cells will span multiple grid cells—but note that every table cell's edges are placed along a grid-cell edge.

These grid cells are largely theoretical constructs, and they cannot be styled or even accessed through the Document Object Model (DOM). They simply serve as a way to describe how tables are assembled for styling.

Table arrangement rules

- Each *row box* encompasses a single row of grid cells. All the row boxes in a table fill the table from top to bottom in the order they occur in the source document (with the exception of any table-header or table-footer row boxes, which come at the beginning and end of the table, respectively). Thus, a table contains as many grid rows as there are row elements (e.g., tr elements).
- A *row group*'s box encompasses the same grid cells as the row boxes it contains.
- A *column box* encompasses one or more columns of grid cells. All the column boxes are placed next to one another in the order they occur. The first column box is on the left for left-to-right languages, and on the right for right-to-left languages.

- A *column group*'s box encompasses the same grid cells as the column boxes it contains.

- Although cells may span several rows or columns, CSS does not define how this happens. It is instead left to the document language to define spanning. Each spanned cell is a rectangular box one or more grid cells wide and high. The top row of this spanning rectangle is in the row that is parent to the spanned grid cell. The cell's rectangle must be as far to the left as possible in left-to-right languages, but it may not overlap any other cell box. It must also be to the right of all cells in the same row that are earlier in the source document (in a left-to-right language). In right-to-left languages, a spanned cell must be as far to the *right* as possible without overlapping other cells, and must be to the *left* of all cells in the same row that follow it in the document source.

- A cell's box *cannot* extend beyond the last row box of a table or row group. If the table structure would cause this condition, the cell must be shortened until it fits within the table or row group that encloses it.

 The CSS specification discourages, but does not prohibit, the positioning of table cells and other internal table elements. Positioning a row that contains row-spanning cells, for example, could dramatically alter the layout of the table by removing the row from the table entirely, thus removing the spanned cells from consideration in the layout of other rows. Nevertheless, it is quite possible to apply positioning to table elements in current browsers.

By definition, grid cells are rectangular, but they do not all have to be the same size. All the grid cells in a given grid column will be the same width, and all the grid cells in a grid row will be the same height, but the height of one grid row may be different than that of another grid row. Similarly, grid columns may be of different widths.

With those basic rules in mind, a question may arise: how, exactly, do you know which elements are cells and which are not?

Table Display Values

In HTML, it's easy to know which elements are parts of tables because the handling of elements like tr and td is built into browsers. In XML, on the other hand, there is no way to intrinsically know which elements might be part of a table. This is where a whole collection of values for display come into play.

display

Values:	none | inline | block | inline-block | list-item | run-in | table | inline-table | table-row-group | table-header-group | table-footer-group | table-row | table-column-group | table-column | table-cell | table-caption | inherit
Initial value:	inline
Applies to:	All elements
Inherited:	No
Computed value:	Varies for floated, positioned, and root elements (see CSS2.1, section 9.7); otherwise, as specified
Note:	The values compact and marker appeared in CSS2, but were dropped from CSS2.1 due to a lack of widespread support.

In this text, we'll stick to the table-related values, as the others (block, inline, inline-block, run-in, and list-item) are beyond the scope of tables. The table-related values can be summarized as follows:

table

> This value specifies that an element defines a block-level table. Thus, it defines a rectangular block that generates a block box. The corresponding HTML element is, not surprisingly, table.

inline-table

> This value specifies that an element defines an inline-level table. This means the element defines a rectangular block that generates an inline box. The closest non-table analogue is the value inline-block. The closest HTML element is table, although, by default, HTML tables are not inline.

table-row

> This value specifies that an element is a row of table cells. The corresponding HTML element is the tr element.

`table-row-group`

> This value specifies that an element groups one or more table rows. The corresponding HTML value is tbody.

`table-header-group`

> This value is very much like `table-row-group`, except that for visual formatting, the header row group is always displayed before all other rows and row groups, and after any top captions. In print, if a table requires multiple pages to print, a user agent may repeat header rows at the top of each page (Firefox does this, for example). The specification does not define what happens if you assign `table-header-group` to multiple elements. A header group can contain multiple rows. The HTML equivalent is thead.

`table-footer-group`

> This value is very much like `table-header-group`, except that the footer row group is always displayed after all other rows and row groups, and before any bottom captions. In print, if a table requires multiple pages to print, a user agent may repeat footer rows at the bottom of each page. The specification does not define what happens if you assign `table-footer-group` to multiple elements. This is equivalent to the HTML element tfoot.

`table-column`

> This value declares that an element describes a column of table cells. In CSS terms, elements with this `display` value are not visually rendered, as if they had the value none. Their existence is largely for the purposes of helping to define the presentation of cells within the column. The HTML equivalent is the col element.

`table-column-group`

> This value declares that an element groups one or more columns. Like `table-column` elements, `table-column-group` elements are not rendered, but the value is useful for defining presentation for elements within the column group. The HTML equivalent is the colgroup element.

`table-cell`

> This value specifies that an element represents a single cell in a table. The HTML elements th and td are both examples of `table-cell` elements.

`table-caption`

> This value defines a table's caption. CSS does not define what should happen if multiple elements have the value caption, but it does explicitly warn, "…authors should not put more than one element with `display: caption` inside a table or inline-table element."

You can get a quick summary of the general effects of these values by taking an excerpt from the example HTML 4.0 stylesheet given in Appendix D of the CSS 2.1 specification:

```
table {display: table;}
tr {display: table-row;}
thead {display: table-header-group;}
tbody {display: table-row-group;}
tfoot {display: table-footer-group;}
col {display: table-column;}
colgroup {display: table-column-group;}
td, th {display: table-cell;}
caption {display: table-caption;}
```

In XML, where elements will not have display semantics by default, these values become quite useful. Consider the following markup:

```
<scores>
    <headers>
        <label>Team</label>
        <label>Score</label>
    </headers>
    <game sport="MLB" league="NL">
        <team>
            <name>Reds</name>
            <score>8</score>
        </team>
        <team>
            <name>Cubs</name>
            <score>5</score>
        </team>
    </game>
</scores>
```

This could be formatted in a tabular fashion using the following styles:

```
scores {display: table;}
headers {display: table-header-group;}
game {display: table-row-group;}
team {display: table-row;}
label, name, score {display: table-cell;}
```

The various cells could then be styled as necessary—for example, boldfacing the label elements and right-aligning the scores.

Row primacy

CSS defines its table model as "row primacy." In other words, the model assumes that authors will create markup languages where rows are explicitly declared. Columns, on the other hand, are derived from the layout of the rows of cells. Thus, the first column is made up of the first cells in each row; the second column is made up of the second cells, and so forth.

Row primacy is not a major issue in HTML, where the markup language is already row-oriented. In XML, it has more of an impact because it constrains the way in which authors can define table markup. Because of the row-oriented nature of the CSS table model, a markup language in which columns are the basis of table layout is not really possible (assuming that the intent is to use CSS to present such documents).

Columns

Although the CSS table model is row-oriented, columns do still play a part in layout. A cell can belong to both contexts (row and column), even though it is descended from row elements in the document source. In CSS, however, columns and column groups can accept only four nontable properties: `border`, `background`, `width`, and `visibility`.

In addition, each of these four properties has special rules that apply only in the columnar context:

border
> Borders can be set for columns and column groups only if the property `border-collapse` has the value `collapse`. In such circumstances, column and column-group borders participate in the collapsing algorithm that sets the border styles at each cell edge. (See the section "Collapsing Cell Borders" on page 20.)

background
> The background of a column or column group will be visible only in cells where both the cell and its row have transparent backgrounds. (See the section "Table Layers" on page 12.)

width
> The `width` property defines the *minimum* width of the column or column group. The content of cells within the column (or group) may force the column to become wider.

visibility
> If the value of `visibility` for a column or column group is `collapse`, then none of the cells in the column (or group) are rendered. Cells that span from the collapsed column into other columns are clipped, as are cells that span from other columns into the hidden column. Furthermore, the overall width of the table is reduced by the width the column would have taken up. A declaration of any `visibility` value other than `hidden` is ignored for a column or column group.

Anonymous Table Objects

There is the possibility that a markup language might not contain enough elements to fully represent tables as they are defined in CSS, or that an author will forget to include all the necessary elements. For example, consider this HTML:

```
<table>
    <td>Name:</td>
    <td><input type="text"></td>
</table>
```

You might glance at this markup and assume that it defines a two-cell table of a single row, but structurally, there is no element defining a row (because the tr is missing).

To cover such possibilities, CSS defines a mechanism for inserting "missing" table components as anonymous objects. For a basic example of how this works, let's revisit our missing-row HTML example. In CSS terms, what effectively happens is that an anonymous table-row object is inserted between the table element and its descendant table cells:

```
<table>
  <!--anonymous table-row object begins-->
    <td>Name:</td>
    <td><input type="text"></td>
  <!--anonymous table-row object ends-->
</table>
```

A visual representation of this process is given in Figure 2, where the dotted line represents the inserted anonymous table row.

Figure 2. Anonymous-object generation in table formatting

Seven different kinds of anonymous-object insertions can occur in the CSS table model. These seven rules are, like inheritance and specificity, an example of a mechanism that attempts to impose intuitive sense on the way CSS behaves.

Object insertion rules

1. If a table-cell element's parent is not a table-row element, then an anonymous table-row object is inserted between the table-cell element and its parent. The

inserted object will include all consecutive siblings of the `table-cell` element. Consider the following styles and markup:

```
system {display: table;}
name, moons {display: table-cell;}

<system>
    <name>Mercury</name>
    <moons>0</moons>
</system>
```

The anonymous `table-row` object is inserted between the cell elements and the `system` element, and it encloses both the `name` and `moons` elements.

The same holds true even if the parent element is a `table-row-group`. To extend the example, assume that the following applies:

```
system {display: table;}
planet {display: table-row-group;}
name, moons {display: table-cell;}

<system>
    <planet>
        <name>Mercury</name>
        <moons>0</moons>
    </planet>
    <planet>
        <name>Venus</name>
        <moons>0</moons>
    </planet>
</system>
```

In this example, both sets of cells will be enclosed in an anonymous `table-row` object that is inserted between them and the `planet` elements.

2. If a `table-row` element's parent is not a `table`, `inline-table`, or `table-row-group` element, then an anonymous `table` element is inserted between the `table-row` element and its parent. The inserted object will include all consecutive siblings of the `table-row` element. Consider the following styles and markup:

```
docbody {display: block;}
planet {display: table-row;}

<docbody>
    <planet>
        <name>Mercury</name>
        <moons>0</moons>
    </planet>
    <planet>
        <name>Venus</name>
        <moons>0</moons>
```

```
        </planet>
    </docbody>
```

Because the display value of the planet elements' parent is block, the anonymous table object is inserted between the planet elements and the docbody element. This anonymous table object will enclose both planet elements, since they are consecutive siblings.

3. If a table-column element's parent is not a table, inline-table, or table-column-group element, then an anonymous table element is inserted between the table-column element and its parent. This is much the same as the table-row rule just discussed, except for its column-oriented nature.

4. If the parent element of a table-row-group, table-header-group, table-footer-group, table-column-group, or table-caption element is not a table element, then an anonymous table object is inserted between the element and its parent.

5. If a child element of a table or inline-table element is not a table-row-group, table-header-group, table-footer-group, table-row, or table-caption element, then an anonymous table-row object is inserted between the table element and its child element. This anonymous object spans all of the consecutive siblings of the child element that are not table-row-group, table-header-group, table-footer-group, table-row, or table-caption elements. Consider the following markup and styles:

```
system {display: table;}
planet {display: table-row;}
name, moons {display: table-cell;}

<system>
    <planet>
        <name>Mercury</name>
        <moons>0</moons>
    </planet>
    <name>Venus</name>
    <moons>0</moons>
</system>
```

Here, a single anonymous table-row object will be inserted between the system element and the second set of name and moons elements. The planet element is not enclosed by the anonymous object because its display is table-row.

6. If a child element of a table-row-group, table-header-group, or table-footer-group element is not a table-row element, then an anonymous table-row object is inserted between the element and its child element. This anonymous object spans all of the consecutive siblings of the child element that are not table-row objects themselves. Consider the following markup and styles:

```
system {display: table;}
planet {display: table-row-group;}
name, moons {display: table-cell;}

<system>
    <planet>
        <name>Mercury</name>
        <moons>0</moons>
    </planet>
    <name>Venus</name>
    <moons>0</moons>
</system>
```

In this case, each set of `name` and `moons` elements will be enclosed in an anonymous `table-row` element. For the second set, the insertion happens in accord with rule 5. For the first set, the anonymous object is inserted between the `planet` element and its children because the `planet` element is a `table-row-group` element.

7. If a child element of a `table-row` element is not a `table-cell` element, then an anonymous `table-cell` object is inserted between the element and its child element. This anonymous object encloses all consecutive siblings of the child element that are not `table-cell` elements themselves. Consider the following markup and styles:

```
system {display: table;}
planet {display: table-row;}
name, moons {display: table-cell;}

<system>
    <planet>
        <name>Mercury</name>
        <num>0</num>
    </planet>
</system>
```

Because the element `num` does not have a table-related `display` value, an anonymous `table-cell` object is inserted between the `planet` element and the `num` element.

This behavior also extends to the encapsulation of anonymous inline boxes. Suppose that the `num` element was not included:

```
<system>
    <planet>
        <name>Mercury</name>
        0
    </planet>
</system>
```

The 0 would still be enclosed in an anonymous `table-cell` object. To further illustrate this point, here is an example adapted from the CSS specification:

```
example {display: table-cell;}
row {display: table-row;}
hey {font-weight: 900;}

<example>
    <row>This is the <hey>top</hey> row.</row>
    <row>This is the <hey>bottom</hey> row.</row>
</example>
```

Within each `row` element, the text fragments and `hey` element are enclosed in anonymous `table-cell` objects.

Table Layers

For the assembly of a table's presentation, CSS defines six individual "layers" on which the various aspects of a table are placed. Figure 3 shows these layers.

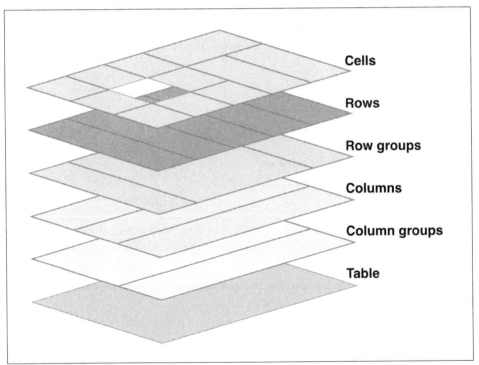

Figure 3. The formatting layers used in table presentation

Basically, the styles for each aspect of the table are drawn on their individual layers. Thus, if the `table` element has a green background and a one-pixel black border, then those styles are drawn on the lowest layer. Any styles for the column groups are drawn on the next layer up, the columns themselves on the layer above that, and so on. The top layer, which corresponds to the table cells, is drawn last.

For the most part, this is simply a logical process; after all, if you declare a background color for table cells, you would want that drawn over the background for the table element. The most important point revealed by Figure 3 is that column styles come below row styles, so a row's background will overwrite a column's background.

It is important to remember that by default, all elements have transparent backgrounds. Thus, in the following markup, the table element's background will be visible "through" cells, rows, columns, and so forth that do not have a background of their own, as illustrated in Figure 4:

```
<table style="background: #B84;">
    <tr>
        <td>hey</td>
        <td style="background: #ABC;">there</td>
    </tr>
    <tr>
        <td>what's</td>
        <td>up?</td>
    </tr>
    <tr style="background: #CBA;">
        <td>not</td>
        <td style="background: #ECC;">much</td>
    </tr>
</table>
```

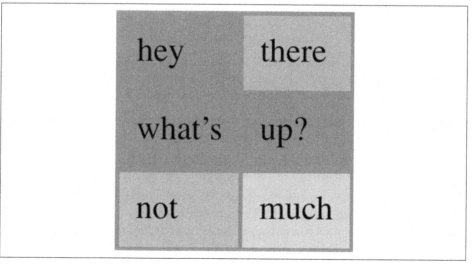

Figure 4. Seeing the background of table-formatting layers through other layers

Captions

A table caption is about what you'd expect: a short bit of text that describes the nature of the table's contents. A chart of stock quotes for the fourth quarter of 2016, therefore, might have a caption element whose contents read "Q4 2016 Stock Performance." With the property caption-side, you can place this element either above or below the table, regardless of where the caption appears in the table's structure. (In HTML5, the caption element can appear only as the first child of a table element, but other languages may have different rules.)

caption-side	
Values:	top | bottom
Initial value:	top
Applies to:	Elements with the display value table-caption
Inherited:	Yes
Computed value:	As specified
Note:	The values left and right appeared in CSS2, but were dropped from CSS2.1 due to a lack of widespread support.

Captions are a bit odd, at least in visual terms. The CSS specification states that a caption is formatted as if it were a block box placed immediately before (or after) the table's box, with one exception: the caption can still inherit values from the table.

A simple example should suffice to illustrate most of the important aspects of caption presentation. Consider the following, illustrated in Figure 5:

```
caption {background: #B84; margin: 1em 0; caption-side: top;}
table {color: white; background: #840; margin: 0.5em 0;}
```

The text in the caption element inherits the color value white from the table, while the caption gets its own background. The separation between the table's outer border edge and the caption's outer margin edge is one em, as the top margin of the table and bottom margin of the caption have collapsed. Finally, the width of the caption is based on the content width of the table element, which is considered to be the containing block of the caption.

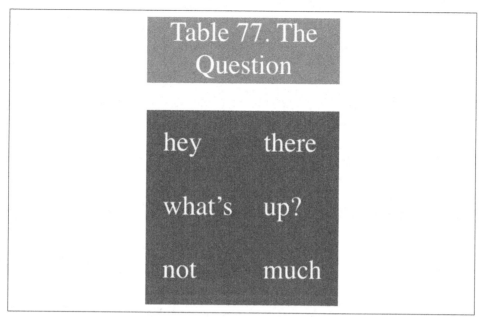

Figure 5. Styling captions and tables

These same results would occur if we change the value of `caption-side` to `bottom`, except that the `caption` would be placed after the table's box, and collapsing would occur between the top margin of the caption and the bottom margin of the table.

For the most part, captions are styled just like any block-level element: they can be padded, have borders, be given backgrounds, and so on. For example, if we need to change the horizontal alignment of text within the caption, we use the property `text-align`. Thus, to right-align the caption in the previous example, we would write:

```
caption {background: gray; margin: 1em 0;
    caption-side: top; text-align: right;}
```

Table Cell Borders

There are two quite distinct border models in CSS. The *separated border model* takes effect when cells are separated from each other in layout terms. The other option is the *collapsed border model*, in which there is no visual separation between cells, and cell borders merge, or collapse into one another. The former is the default model, although in an earlier version of CSS the latter was the default.

An author can choose between the two models with the property `border-collapse`.

The whole point of this property is to offer a way to determine which border model the user agent will employ. If the value collapse is in effect, then the collapsing borders model is used. If the value is separate, then the separated borders model is used. We'll look at the latter model first, since it's much simpler to describe, and it's the default value.

Separated Cell Borders

In this model, every cell in the table is separated from the other cells by some distance, and the borders of cells do not collapse into one another. Thus, given the following styles and markup, you would see the result shown in Figure 6:

```
table {border-collapse: separate;}
td {border: 3px double black; padding: 3px;}
tr:nth-child(2) td:nth-child(2) {border-color: gray;}

<table cellspacing="0">
    <tr>
        <td>cell one</td>
        <td>cell two</td>
    </tr>
    <tr>
        <td>cell three</td>
        <td>cell four</td>
    </tr>
</table>
```

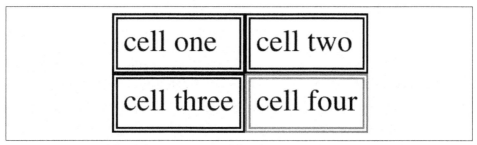

Figure 6. Separated (and thus separate) cell borders

Note that the cell borders touch but remain distinct from one another. The three lines between cells are actually the two double borders sitting right next to each other; the gray border around the fourth cell helps make this more clear.

The HTML attribute `cellspacing` was included in the preceding example to make sure the cells had no separation between them, but its presence is likely a bit troubling. After all, if you can define that borders be separate, then there ought to be a way to use CSS to alter the spacing between cells. Fortunately, there is.

Border spacing

Once you've separated the table cell borders, there may be situations where you want those borders to be separated by some distance. This can be easily accomplished with the property `border-spacing`, which provides a more powerful replacement for the HTML attribute `cellspacing`.

border-spacing

Values:	`<length> <length>?` | `inherit`
Initial value:	0
Applies to:	Elements with the display value `table` or `table-inline`
Inherited:	Yes
Computed value:	Two absolute lengths
Note:	Property is ignored unless `border-collapse` value is `separate`

Either one or two lengths can be given for the value of this property. If you want all your cells separated by a single pixel, then border-spacing: 1px; will suffice. If, on the other hand, you want cells to be separated by one pixel horizontally and five pixels vertically, write border-spacing: 1px 5px;. If two lengths are supplied, the first is always the horizontal separation, and the second is always the vertical.

The spacing values are also applied between the borders of cells along the outside of a table and the padding on the table element itself. Given the following styles, you would get the result shown in Figure 7:

```
table {border-collapse: separate; border-spacing: 5px 8px;
padding: 12px; border: 2px solid black;}
td { border: 1px solid gray;}
td#squeeze {border-width: 5px;}
```

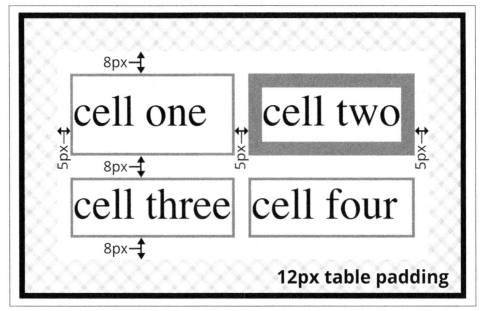

Figure 7. Border spacing effects between cells and their enclosing table

In Figure 7, there is a space 5 pixels wide between the borders of any two horizontally adjacent cells, and there are 17 pixels of space between the borders of the right- and left-most cells and the right and left borders of the table element. Similarly, the borders of vertically adjacent cells are 8 pixels apart, and the borders of the cells in the top and bottom rows are 20 pixels from the top and bottom borders of the table, respectively. The separation between cell borders is constant throughout the table, regardless of the border widths of the cells themselves.

Note also that if you're going to declare a `border-spacing` value, it's done on the table itself, not on the individual cells. If `border-spacing` had been declared for the `td` elements in the previous example, it would have been ignored.

In the separated-border model, borders cannot be set for rows, row groups, columns, and column groups. Any border properties declared for such elements must be ignored by a CSS-conformant user agent.

Handling empty cells

Because every cell is, in a visual sense, distinct from all the other cells in the table, what do you do with cells that are empty (i.e., have no content)? You have two choices, which are reflected in the values of the `empty-cells` property.

<table>
<tr><td colspan="2" align="center">empty-cells</td></tr>
<tr><td>Values:</td><td>show | hide | inherit</td></tr>
<tr><td>Initial value:</td><td>show</td></tr>
<tr><td>Applies to:</td><td>Elements with the display value table-cell</td></tr>
<tr><td>Inherited:</td><td>Yes</td></tr>
<tr><td>Computed value:</td><td>As specified</td></tr>
<tr><td>Note:</td><td>Property is ignored unless border-collapse value is separate.</td></tr>
</table>

If `empty-cells` is set to `show`, then the borders and background of an empty cell will be drawn, just as with table cells that have content. If the value is `hide`, then no part of the cell is drawn, just as if the cell were set to `visibility: hidden`.

If a cell contains any content, it cannot be considered empty. "Content," in this case, includes not only text, images, form elements, and so on, but also the nonbreaking space entity (` `) and any other whitespace *except* the CR (carriage return), LF (linefeed), tab, and space characters. If all the cells in a row are empty, and all have an `empty-cells` value of `hide`, then the entire row is treated as if the row element were set to `display: none`.

Collapsing Cell Borders

While the collapsing cell model largely describes how HTML tables have always been laid out when they don't have any cell spacing, it is quite a bit more complicated than the separated borders model. There are also some rules that set collapsing cell borders apart from the separated borders model. These are:

- Elements with a `display` of `table` or `inline-table` cannot have any padding when `border-collapse` is `collapse`, although they can have margins. Thus, there is never separation between the border around the outside of the table and the edges of its outermost cells in the collapsed borders model.
- Borders can be applied to cells, rows, row groups, columns, and column groups. A table itself can, as always, have a border.
- There is never any separation between cell borders in the collapsed borders model. In fact, borders collapse into each other where they adjoin, so that only one of the collapsing borders is actually drawn. This is somewhat akin to margin collapsing, where the largest margin wins. When cell borders collapse, the "most interesting" border wins.
- Once they are collapsed, the borders between cells are centered on the hypothetical grid lines between the cells.

We'll explore the last two points in more detail in the next two sections.

Collapsing border layout

In order to better understand how the collapsing borders model works, let's look at the layout of a single table row, as shown in Figure 8.

For each cell, the padding and content width of the cell is inside the borders, as expected. For the borders between cells, half of the border is to one side of the grid line between two cells, and the other half is to the other side. In each case, only a single border is drawn along each cell edge. You might think that half of each cell's border is drawn to each side of the grid line, but that's not what happens.

For example, assume that the solid borders on the middle cell are green and the solid borders on the outer two cells are red. The borders on the right and left sides of the middle cell (which collapse with the adjacent borders of the outer cells) will be all green, or all red, depending on which border wins out. We'll discuss how to tell which one wins in the next section.

You may have noticed that the outer borders protrude past the table's width. This is because in this model, *half* the table's borders are included in the width. The other half sticks out beyond that distance, sitting in the margin itself. This might seem a bit weird, but that's how the model is defined to work.

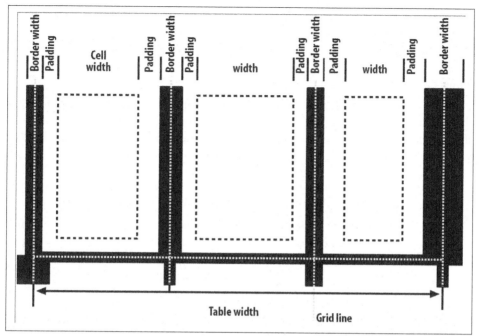

Figure 8. The layout of a table row using the collapsing borders model

The specification includes a layout formula that I'll reproduce here for the benefit of those who enjoy such things:

row width = (0.5 * border-width-0) + padding-left-1 + width-1 + padding-right-1 + border-width-1 + padding-left-2 +...+ padding-right-n + (0.5 * border-width-n)

Each `border-width-`n refers to the border between cell n and the next cell; thus, `border-width-3` refers to the border between the third and fourth cells. The value n stands for the total number of cells in the row.

There is a slight exception to this mechanism. When beginning the layout of a collapsed-border table, the user agent computes an initial left and right border for the table itself. It does this by examining the left border of the first cell in the first row of the table and by taking half of that border's width as the table's initial left border width. The user agent then examines the right border of the last cell in the first row and uses half that width to set the table's initial right-border width. For any row after the first, if the left or right border is wider than the initial border widths, it sticks out into the margin area of the table.

In cases where a border is an odd number of display elements (pixels, printer dots, etc.) wide, the user agent is left to decide what to do about centering the border on the grid line. It might shift the border so that it is slightly off-center, round up or down to an even number of display elements, use anti-aliasing, or adjust anything else that seems reasonable.

Border collapsing

When two or more borders are adjacent, they collapse into each other. In fact, they don't collapse so much as fight it out to see which of them will gain supremacy over the others. There are some strict rules governing which borders will win and which will not:

- If one of the collapsing borders has a border-style of hidden, it takes precedence over all other collapsing borders. All borders at this location are hidden.

- If all the borders are visible, then wider borders take precedence over narrower ones. Thus, if a two-pixel dotted border and a five-pixel double border collapse, the border at that location will be a five-pixel double border.

- If all collapsing borders have the same width but different border styles, then the border style is taken in the following order, from most to least preferred: double, solid, dashed, dotted, ridge, outset, groove, inset, none. Thus, if two borders with the same width are collapsing, and one is dashed while the other is outset, the border at that location will be dashed.

- If collapsing borders have the same style and width, but differ in color, then the color used is taken from an element in the following list, from most preferred to least: cell, row, row group, column, column group, table. Thus, if the borders of a cell and a column (identical in every way except color) collapse, then the cell's border color (and style and width) will be used. If the collapsing borders come from the same type of element, such as two row borders with the same style and width but different colors, then the color is taken from borders that are further to the top and left (in left-to-right languages; otherwise, further to the top and right).

The following styles and markup, presented in Figure 9, help illustrate each of the four rules:

```
table {border-collapse: collapse;
border: 3px outset gray;}
td {border: 1px solid gray; padding: 0.5em;}
#r2c1, #r2c2 {border-style: hidden;}
#r1c1, #r1c4 {border-width: 5px;}
#r2c4 {border-style: double; border-width: 3px;}
#r3c4 {border-style: dotted; border-width: 2px;}
#r4c1 {border-bottom-style: hidden;}
#r4c3 {border-top: 13px solid silver;}
```

```
<table>
    <tr>
        <td id="r1c1">1-1</td>
        <td id="r1c2">1-2</td>
        <td id="r1c3">1-3</td>
        <td id="r1c4">1-4</td>
    </tr>
    <tr>
        <td id="r2c1">2-1</td>
        <td id="r2c2">2-2</td>
        <td id="r2c3">2-3</td>
        <td id="r2c4">2-4</td>
    </tr>
    <tr>
        <td id="r3c1">3-1</td>
        <td id="r3c2">3-2</td>
        <td id="r3c3">3-3</td>
        <td id="r3c4">3-4</td>
    </tr>
    <tr>
        <td id="r4c1">4-1</td>
        <td id="r4c2">4-2</td>
        <td id="r4c3">4-3</td>
        <td id="r4c4">4-4</td>
    </tr>
</table>
```

Let's consider what happened for each of the cells, in turn:

- For cells 1-1 and 1-4, the five-pixel borders were wider than any of their adjacent borders, so they won out not only over adjoining cell borders, but over the border of the table itself. The only exception is the bottom of cell 1-1, which was suppressed.

- The bottom border on cell 1-1 was suppressed because cells 2-1 and 2-2, with their explicitly hidden borders, completely remove any borders from the edge of the cells. Again, the table's border lost out (on the left edge of cell 2-1) to a cell's border. The bottom border of cell 4-1 was also hidden, and so it prevented any border from appearing below the cell.

- The three-pixel double border of cell 2-4 was overridden on top by the five-pixel solid border of cell 1-4. Cell 2-4's border, in turn, overrode the border between itself and cell 2-3 because it was both wider and "more interesting." Cell 2-4 also overrode the border between itself and cell 3-4, even though both are the same width, because 2-4's double style is defined to be "more interesting" than 3-4's dotted border.

- The 13-pixel bottom silver border of cell 3-3 not only overrode the top border of cell 4-3, but it also affected the layout of content within both cells *and* the rows that contain both cells.

- For cells along the outer edge of the table that aren't specially styled, their one-pixel solid borders are overridden by the three-pixel outset border on the table element itself.

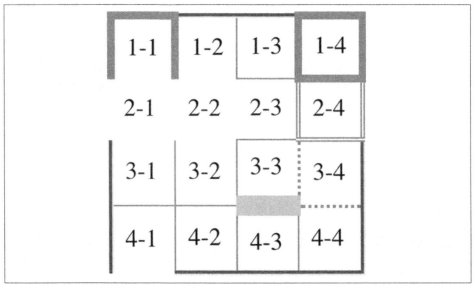

Figure 9. Manipulating border widths, styles, and colors leads to some unusual results

This is, in fact, about as complicated as it sounds, although the behaviors are largely intuitive and make a little more sense with practice. It's worth noting, though, that the basic Netscape 1.1-era table presentation can be captured with a fairly simple set of rules, described here and illustrated by Figure 10:

```
table {border-collapse: collapse; border: 2px outset gray;}
td {border: 1px inset gray;}
```

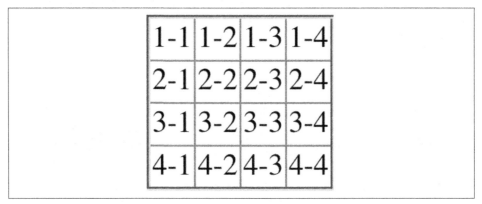

Figure 10. Reproducing old-school table presentation

Table Sizing

Now that we've dug into the guts of table formatting and cell border appearance, we have the pieces we need to understand the sizing of tables and their internal elements. When it comes to determining table width, there are two different approaches: *fixed-width layout* and *automatic-width layout*. Heights are calculated automatically no matter what width algorithms are used.

Width

Since there are two different ways to figure out the width of a table, it's only logical that there be a way to declare which should be used for a given table. Authors can use the property `table-layout` to select between the two kinds of table width calculation.

table-layout	
Values:	`auto`|`fixed`|`inherit`
Initial value:	`auto`
Applies to:	Elements with the `display` value `table` or `inline-table`
Inherited:	Yes
Computed value:	As specified

While the two models can have different results in laying out a given table, the fundamental difference between the two is that of speed. With a fixed-width table layout, the user agent can calculate the layout of the table more quickly than is possible in the automatic-width model.

Fixed layout

The main reason the fixed-layout model is so fast is that its layout does not depend on the contents of table cells. Instead, it's driven by the width values of the table, columns, and cells within that table.

The fixed-layout model works in the following simple steps:

1. Any column element whose `width` property has a value other than `auto` sets the width for that entire column.

a. If a column has an `auto` width, but the cell in the first row of the table within that column has a `width` other than `auto`, then the cell sets the width for that entire column. If the cell spans multiple columns, then the width is divided between the columns.

b. Any columns that are still auto-sized are sized so that their widths are as equal as possible.

At that point, the width of the table is set to be either the value of `width` for the table or the sum of the column widths, whichever is *greater*. If the table turns out to be wider than its columns, then the difference is divided by the number of columns and the result is added to each of them.

This approach is fast because all of the column widths are defined by the first row of the table. The cells in any rows that come after the first are sized according to the column widths that were defined by the first row. The cells in those following rows do not—indeed, cannot—change column widths, which means that any `width` value assigned to those cells will be ignored. In cases where a cell's content does not fit into its cell, the `overflow` value for the cell determines whether the cell contents are clipped, visible, or generate a scrollbar.

Let's consider the following styles and markup, which are illustrated in Figure 11:

```
table {table-layout: fixed; width: 400px;
    border-collapse: collapse;}
td {border: 1px solid;}
col#c1 {width: 200px;}
#r1c2 {width: 75px;}
#r2c3 {width: 500px;}

<table>
    <colgroup> <col id="c1"><col id="c2"><col id="c3"><col id="c4"> </colgroup>
    <tr>
        <td id="r1c1">1-1</td>
        <td id="r1c2">1-2</td>
        <td id="r1c3">1-3</td>
        <td id="r1c4">1-4</td>
    </tr>
    <tr>
        <td id="r2c1">2-1</td>
        <td id="r2c2">2-2</td>
        <td id="r2c3">2-3</td>
        <td id="r2c4">2-4</td>
    </tr>
    <tr>
        <td id="r3c1">3-1</td>
        <td id="r3c2">3-2</td>
        <td id="r3c3">3-3</td>
        <td id="r3c4">3-4</td>
    </tr>
```

```
  <tr>
      <td id="r4c1">4-1</td>
      <td id="r4c2">4-2</td>
      <td id="r4c3">4-3</td>
      <td id="r4c4">4-4</td>
  </tr>
</table>
```

200px		75px	61px	61px
1-1		1-2	1-3	1-4
2-1		2-2	2-3	2-4
3-1		3-2	3-3	3-4
4-1		4-2	4-3	4-4

Figure 11. Fixed-width table layout

As you can see in Figure 11, the first column is 200 pixels wide, which happens to be half the 400-pixel width of the table. The second column is 75 pixels wide, because the first-row cell within that column has been assigned an explicit width. The third and fourth columns are each 61 pixels wide. Why? Because the sum of the column widths for the first and second columns (275 pixels), plus the various borders between columns (3 pixels), equals 278 pixels. 400 minus 278 is 122, and that divided in half is 61, so that's how many pixels wide the third and fourth columns will be. What about the 500-pixel width for #r2c3? It's ignored because that cell isn't in the first row of the table.

Note that it is not absolutely necessary that the table have an explicit width value to make use of the fixed-width layout model, although it definitely helps. For example, given the following, a user agent could calculate a width for the table that is 50 pixels narrower than the parent element's width. It would then use that calculated width in the fixed-layout algorithm:

```
table {table-layout: fixed; margin: 0 25px; width: auto;}
```

This is not required, however. User agents are also permitted to lay out any table with an auto value for width using the automatic-width layout model.

Automatic layout

The automatic-width layout model, while not as fast as fixed layout, is probably much more familiar to you because it's substantially the same model that HTML tables have used for years. In most current user agents, use of this model will be triggered by a table having a `width` of `auto`, regardless of the value of `table-layout`, although this is not assured.

The reason automatic layout is slower is that the table cannot be laid out until the user agent has looked at all of the content in the table. That is, it requires that the user agent lay out the entire table in a fashion that takes the contents and styles of every cell into account. This generally requires the user agent to perform some calculations and then go back through the table to perform a second set of calculations.

The content has to be fully examined because, as with HTML tables, the table's layout is dependent on the content in all the cells. If there is a 400-pixel-wide image in a cell in the last row, then it will force all of the cells above it (those in the same column) to be at least 400 pixels wide. Thus, the width of every cell has to be calculated, and adjustments must be made (possibly triggering another round of content-width calculations) before the table can be laid out.

The details of the model can be expressed in the following steps:

1. For each cell in a column, calculate both the minimum and maximum cell width.

   a. Determine the minimum width required to display the content. In determining this minimum content width, the content can flow to any number of lines, but it may not stick out of the cell's box. If the cell has a `width` value that is larger than the minimum possible width, then the minimum cell width is set to the value of `width`. If the cell's `width` value is `auto`, then the minimum cell width is set to the minimum content width.

   b. For the maximum width, determine the width required to display the content without any line breaking other than that forced by explicit line breaking (e.g., the `<br>` element). That value is the maximum cell width.

2. For each column, calculate both the minimum and maximum column width.

   a. The column's minimum width is determined by the largest minimum cell width of the cells within the column. If the column has been given an explicit `width` value that is larger than any of the minimum cell widths within the column, then the minimum column width is set to the value of `width`.

   b. For the maximum width, take the largest maximum cell width of the cells within the column. If the column has been given an explicit `width` value that is larger than any of the maximum cell widths within the column, then the maximum column width is set to the value of `width`. These two behaviors recreate the traditional HTML table behavior of forcibly expanding any column to be as wide as its widest cell.

3. In cases where a cell spans more than one column, then the sum of the minimum column widths must be equal to the minimum cell width for the spanning cell. Similarly, the sum of the maximum column widths has to equal the spanning

cell's maximum width. User agents should divide any changes in column widths equally among the spanned columns.

In addition, the user agent must take into account that when a column width has a percentage value for its width, the percentage is calculated in relation to the width of the table—even though it doesn't yet know what that will be! It instead has to hang on to the percentage value and use it in the next part of the algorithm.

At this point, the user agent will have figured how wide or narrow each column *can* be. With that information in hand, it can then proceed to actually figuring out the width of the table. This happens as follows:

1. If the computed width of the table is not `auto`, then the computed table width is compared to the sum of all the column widths *plus* any borders and cell spacing. (Columns with percentage widths are likely calculated at this time.) The larger of the two is the final width of the table. If the table's computed width is *larger* than the sum of the column widths, borders, and cell spacing, then the difference is divided by the number of columns and the result is added to each of them.

2. If the computed width of the table is `auto`, then the final width of the table is determined by adding up the column widths, borders, and cell spacing. This means that the table will be only as wide as needed to display its content, just as with traditional HTML tables. Any columns with percentage widths use that percentage as a constraint—but one that a user agent does not have to satisfy.

Once the last step is completed, then—and only then—can the user agent actually lay out the table.

The following styles and markup, presented in Figure 12, help illustrate how this process works:

```
table {table-layout: auto; width: auto;
    border-collapse: collapse;}
td {border: 1px solid; padding: 0;}
col#c3 {width: 25%;}
#r1c2 {width: 40%;}
#r2c2 {width: 50px;}
#r2c3 {width: 35px;}
#r4c1 {width: 100px;}
#r4c4 {width: 1px;}

<table>
    <colgroup> <col id="c1"><col id="c2"><col id="c3"><col id="c4"> </colgroup>
    <tr>
        <td id="r1c1">1-1</td>
        <td id="r1c2">1-2</td>
        <td id="r1c3">1-3</td>
        <td id="r1c4">1-4</td>
    </tr>
```

```
    <tr>
        <td id="r2c1">2-1</td>
        <td id="r2c2">2-2</td>
        <td id="r2c3">2-3</td>
        <td id="r2c4">2-4</td>
    </tr>
    <tr>
        <td id="r3c1">3-1</td>
        <td id="r3c2">3-2</td>
        <td id="r3c3">3-3</td>
        <td id="r3c4">3-4</td>
    </tr>
    <tr>
        <td id="r4c1">4-1</td>
        <td id="r4c2">4-2</td>
        <td id="r4c3">4-3</td>
        <td id="r4c4">4-4</td>
    </tr>
</table>
```

100px	141px	88px	22px
1-1	1-2	1-3	1-4
2-1	2-2	2-3	2-4
3-1	3-2	3-3	3-4
4-1	4-2	4-3	4-4

Figure 12. Automatic table layout

Let's consider what happened for each of the columns, in turn:

- For the first column, the only explicit cell or column width is that of cell 4-1, which was given a width of 100px. Because the content is so short, both the minimum and maximum column widths are set to 100px. (If there were a cell in the column with several sentences of text, it would have increased the maximum column width to whatever width necessary to display all of the text without line-breaking.)

- For the second column, two widths were declared: cell 1-2 was given a width of 40%, and cell 2-2 was given a width of 50px. The minimum width of this column is 50px, and the maximum width is 40% of the final table width.

- For the third column, only cell 3-3 had an explicit width (35px), but the column itself was given a width of 25%. Therefore, the minimum column width is 35 pixels, and the maximum width is 25% of the final table width.

- For the fourth column, only cell 4-4 was given an explicit width (1px). This is smaller than the minimum content width, so both the minimum and maximum column widths are equal to the minimum content width of the cells. This turns out to be a computed 22 pixels, so the minimum and maximum widths are both 22 pixels.

The user agent now knows that the four columns have minimum and maximum widths as follows:

- Minimum 100px, maximum 100px
  — Minimum 50px, maximum 40%
  — Minimum 35px, maximum 25%
  — Minimum 25px, maximum 22px

Thus, the table's minimum width is the sum of all the column minimums, plus the borders collapsed between the columns, which totals 215 pixels. The table's maximum width is 123px + 65%, where the 123px comes from the first and last columns and their shares of the collapsed borders. This maximum works out to be 351.42857142857143 pixels (given that 123px represents 35% of the overall table width). With this number in hand, the second column will be 140.5 pixels wide, and the third column will be 87.8 pixels wide. These may be rounded by the user agent to whole numbers such as 141px and 88px, or not, depending on the exact rendering method used. (These are the numbers used in Figure 12.)

Note that it is not required that user agents actually use the maximum value; they may choose another course of action.

Of course, this was (although it may not seem like it) a very simple and straightforward example: all of the content was basically the same width, and most of the declared widths were pixel lengths. In a situation where a table contains images, paragraphs of text, form elements, and so forth, the process of figuring out the table's layout is likely to be a great deal more complicated.

Height

After all of the effort that was expended in figuring out the width of the table, you might well wonder how much more complicated height calculation will be. Actually, in CSS terms, it's pretty simple, although browser developers probably don't think so.

The easiest situation to describe is one in which the table height is explicitly set via the height property. In such cases, the height of the table is defined by the value of height. This means that a table may be taller or shorter than the sum of its row heights. Note that height is treated much more like min-height for tables, so if you define a height value that's smaller than the sum total of the row heights, it may appear to be ignored.

By contrast, if the height value of a table is greater than the total of its row heights, the specification explicitly refuses to define what should happen, instead noting that the issue may be resolved in future versions of CSS. A user agent could expand the table's rows to fill out its height, or leave blank space inside the table's box, or something completely different. It's up to each user agent to decide.

 As of mid-2016, the most common behavior of user agents was to increase the heights of the rows in a table to fill out its overall height. This was accomplished by taking the difference between the table height and the sum of the row heights, dividing it by the number of rows, and applying the resulting amount to each row.

If the height of the table is auto, then its height is the sum of the heights of all the rows within the table, plus any borders and cell spacing. To determine the height of each row, the user agent goes through a process similar to that used to find the widths of columns. It calculates a minimum and maximum height for the contents of each cell and then uses these to derive a minimum and maximum height for the row. After having done this for all the rows, the user agent figures out what each row's height should be, stacks them all on top of one another, and uses the total to determine the table's height. It's a lot like inline layout, only with less certainty in how things should be done.

In addition to what to do about tables with explicit heights and how to treat row heights within them, you can add the following to the list of things CSS does not define:

- The effect of a percentage height for table cells.
- The effect of a percentage height for table rows and row groups.
- How a row-spanning cell affects the heights of the rows that are spanned, except that the rows have to contain the spanning cell.

As you can see, height calculations in tables are largely left up to user agents to figure out. Historical evidence would suggest that this will lead to each user agent doing something different, so you should probably avoid setting table heights as much as possible.

Alignment

In a rather interesting turn of events, alignment of content within cells is a lot better defined than cell and row heights. This is true even for vertical alignment, which can quite easily affect the height of a row.

Horizontal alignment is the simplest. To align content within a cell, you use the `text-align` property. In effect, the cell is treated as a block-level box, and all of the content within it is aligned as per the `text-align` value.

To vertically align content in a table cell, `vertical-align` is the relevant property. It uses many of the same values that are used for vertically aligning inline content, but the meanings of those values change when applied to a table cell. To summarize the three simplest cases:

top
> The top of the cell's content is aligned with the top of its row; in the case of row-spanning cells, the top of the cell's content is aligned with the top of the first row it spans.

bottom
> The bottom of the cell's content is aligned with the bottom of its row; in the case of row-spanning cells, the bottom of the cell's content is aligned with the bottom of the last row it spans.

middle
> The middle of the cell's content is aligned with the middle of its row; in the case of row-spanning cells, the middle of the cell's content is aligned with the middle of all the rows it spans.

These are illustrated in Figure 13, which uses the following styles and markup:

```
table {table-layout: auto; width: 20em;
border-collapse: separate; border-spacing: 3px;}
td {border: 1px solid; background: silver;
    padding: 0;}
div {border: 1px dashed gray; background: white;}
#r1c1 {vertical-align: top; height: 10em;}
#r1c2 {vertical-align: middle;}
#r1c3 {vertical-align: bottom;}

<table>
    <tr>
        <td id="r1c1">
        <div>
            The contents of this cell are top-aligned.
        </div>
        </td>
        <td id="r1c2">
```

```
            <div>
                The contents of this cell are middle-aligned.
            </div>
            </td>
            <td id="r1c3">
            <div>
                The contents of this cell are bottom-aligned.
            </div>
            </td>
        </tr>
    </table>
```

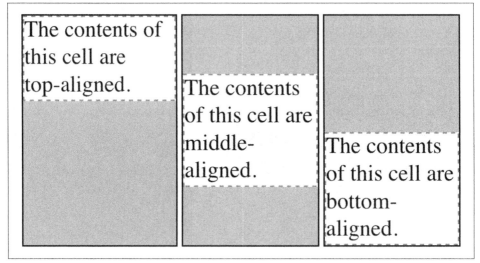

Figure 13. Vertical alignment of cell contents

In each case, the alignment is carried out by automatically increasing the padding of the cell itself to achieve the desired effect. In the first cell in Figure 13, the bottom padding of the cell has been changed to equal the difference between the height of the cell's box and the height of the content within the cell. For the second cell, the top and bottom padding of the cell have been reset to be equal, thus vertically centering the content of the cell. In the last cell, the cell's top padding has been altered.

The fourth possible value alignment is baseline, and it's a little more complicated that the first three:

baseline
> The baseline of the cell is aligned with the baseline of its row; in the case of row-spanning cells, the baseline of the cell is aligned with the baseline of the first row it spans.

It's easiest to provide an illustration (Figure 14) and then discuss what's happening.

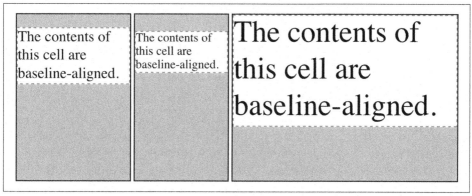

Figure 14. Baseline alignment of cell contents

A row's baseline is defined by the lowest initial cell baseline (that is, the baseline of the first line of text) out of all its cells. Thus, in Figure 14, the row's baseline was defined by the third cell, which has the lowest initial baseline. The first two cells then have the baseline of their first line of text aligned with the row's baseline.

As with top, middle, and bottom alignment, the placement of baseline-aligned cell content is accomplished by altering the top and bottom padding of the cells. In cases where none of the cells in a row are baseline-aligned, the row does not even have a baseline—it doesn't really need one.

The detailed process for aligning cell contents within a row is as follows:

1. If any of the cells are baseline-aligned, then the row's baseline is determined and the content of the baseline-aligned cells is placed.

   a. Any top-aligned cell has its content placed. The row now has a provisional height, which is defined by the lowest cell bottom of the cells that have already had their content placed.

   b. If any remaining cells are middle- or bottom-aligned, and the content height is taller than the provisional row height, the height of the row is increased to enclose the tallest of those cells.

   c. All remaining cells have their content placed. In any cell whose contents are shorter than the row height, the cell's padding is increased in order to match the height of the row.

The `vertical-align` values `sub`, `super`, `text-top`, and `text-bottom` are supposed to be ignored when applied to table cells. Instead, they seem to all treated as if they are `baseline`, or possibly `top`.

Summary

Even if you're quite familiar with table layout from years of table-and-spacer design, it turns out that the mechanisms driving such layout are rather complicated. Thanks to the legacy of HTML table construction, the CSS table model is row-centric, but it does, thankfully, accommodate columns and limited column styling. Thanks to new abilities to affect cell alignment and table width, you now have even more tools for presenting tables in a pleasing way.

The ability to apply table-related display values to arbitrary elements opens the door to creating table-like layouts using HTML elements such as div and section, or in XML languages where any element could be used to describe table components.

About the Author

Eric A. Meyer has been working with the Web since late 1993 and is an internationally recognized expert on the subjects of HTML, CSS, and web standards. A widely read author, he is also the founder of Complex Spiral Consulting (*http://www.complex spiral.com*), which counts among its clients America Online; Apple Computer, Inc.; Wells Fargo Bank; and Macromedia, which described Eric as "a critical partner in our efforts to transform Macromedia Dreamweaver MX 2004 into a revolutionary tool for CSS-based design."

Beginning in early 1994, Eric was the visual designer and campus web coordinator for the Case Western Reserve University website, where he also authored a widely acclaimed series of three HTML tutorials and was project coordinator for the online version of the *Encyclopedia of Cleveland History* and the *Dictionary of Cleveland Biography*, the first encyclopedia of urban history published fully and freely on the Web.

Author of *Eric Meyer on CSS* and *More Eric Meyer on CSS* (New Riders), *CSS: The Definitive Guide* (*http://bit.ly/css-tdg-3e*) (O'Reilly), and *CSS 2.0 Programmer's Reference* (Osborne/McGraw-Hill), as well as numerous articles for the O'Reilly Network, Web Techniques, and Web Review, Eric also created the CSS Browser Compatibility Charts and coordinated the authoring and creation of the W3C's official CSS Test Suite. He has lectured to a wide variety of organizations, including Los Alamos National Laboratory, the New York Public Library, Cornell University, and the University of Northern Iowa. Eric has also delivered addresses and technical presentations at numerous conferences, among them An Event Apart (which he cofounded), the IW3C2 WWW series, Web Design World, CMP, SXSW, the User Interface conference series, and The Other Dreamweaver Conference.

In his personal time, Eric acts as list chaperone of the highly active css-discuss mailing list (*http://www.css-discuss.org*), which he cofounded with John Allsopp of Western Civilisation, and which is now supported by *evolt.org*. Eric lives in Cleveland, Ohio, which is a much nicer city than you've been led to believe. For nine years he was the host of "Your Father's Oldsmobile," a big-band radio show heard weekly on WRUW 91.1 FM in Cleveland.

You can find more detailed information on Eric's personal web page (*http://www.meyerweb.com/eric*).

Colophon

The animals on the cover of *Table Layout in CSS* are salmon (*salmonidae*), which is a family of fish consisting of many different species. Two of the most common salmon are the Pacific salmon and the Atlantic salmon.

Pacific salmon live in the northern Pacific Ocean off the coasts of North America and Asia. There are five subspecies of Pacific salmon, with an average weight of 10 to 30 pounds. Pacific salmon are born in the fall in freshwater stream gravel beds, where they incubate through the winter and emerge as inch-long fish. They live for a year or two in streams or lakes and then head downstream to the ocean. There they live for a few years, before heading back upstream to their exact place of birth to spawn and then die.

Atlantic salmon live in the northern Atlantic Ocean off the coasts of North America and Europe. There are many subspecies of Atlantic salmon, including the trout and the char. Their average weight is 10 to 20 pounds. The Atlantic salmon family has a life cycle similar to that of its Pacific cousins, and also travels from freshwater gravel beds to the sea. A major difference between the two, however, is that the Atlantic salmon does not die after spawning; it can return to the ocean and then return to the stream to spawn again, usually two or three times.

Salmon, in general, are graceful, silver-colored fish with spots on their backs and fins. Their diet consists of plankton, insect larvae, shrimp, and smaller fish. Their unusually keen sense of smell is thought to help them navigate from the ocean back to the exact spot of their birth, upstream past many obstacles. Some species of salmon remain landlocked, living their entire lives in freshwater.

Salmon are an important part of the ecosystem, as their decaying bodies provide fertilizer for streambeds. Their numbers have been dwindling over the years, however. Factors in the declining salmon population include habitat destruction, fishing, dams that block spawning paths, acid rain, droughts, floods, and pollution.

Many of the animals on O'Reilly covers are endangered; all of them are important to the world. To learn more about how you can help, go to *animals.oreilly.com*.

The cover image is a 19th-century engraving from the Dover Pictorial Archive. The cover fonts are URW Typewriter and Guardian Sans. The text font is Adobe Minion Pro; the heading font is Adobe Myriad Condensed; and the code font is Dalton Maag's Ubuntu Mono.

Get even more for your money.

Join the O'Reilly Community, and register the O'Reilly books you own. It's free, and you'll get:

- $4.99 ebook upgrade offer
- 40% upgrade offer on O'Reilly print books
- Membership discounts on books and events
- Free lifetime updates to ebooks and videos
- Multiple ebook formats, DRM FREE
- Participation in the O'Reilly community
- Newsletters
- Account management
- 100% Satisfaction Guarantee

Signing up is easy:

1. Go to: oreilly.com/go/register
2. Create an O'Reilly login.
3. Provide your address.
4. Register your books.

Note: English-language books only

To order books online:
oreilly.com/store

For questions about products or an order:
orders@oreilly.com

To sign up to get topic-specific email announcements and/or news about upcoming books, conferences, special offers, and new technologies:
elists@oreilly.com

For technical questions about book content:
booktech@oreilly.com

To submit new book proposals to our editors:
proposals@oreilly.com

O'Reilly books are available in multiple DRM-free ebook formats. For more information:
oreilly.com/ebooks

CPSIA information can be obtained at www.ICGtesting.com
Printed in the USA
BVOW09s2149240616

453417BV00004B/4/P